Fantastic
ANIMALS

GRAYSCALE COLORING BOOKS

VOLUME 2.

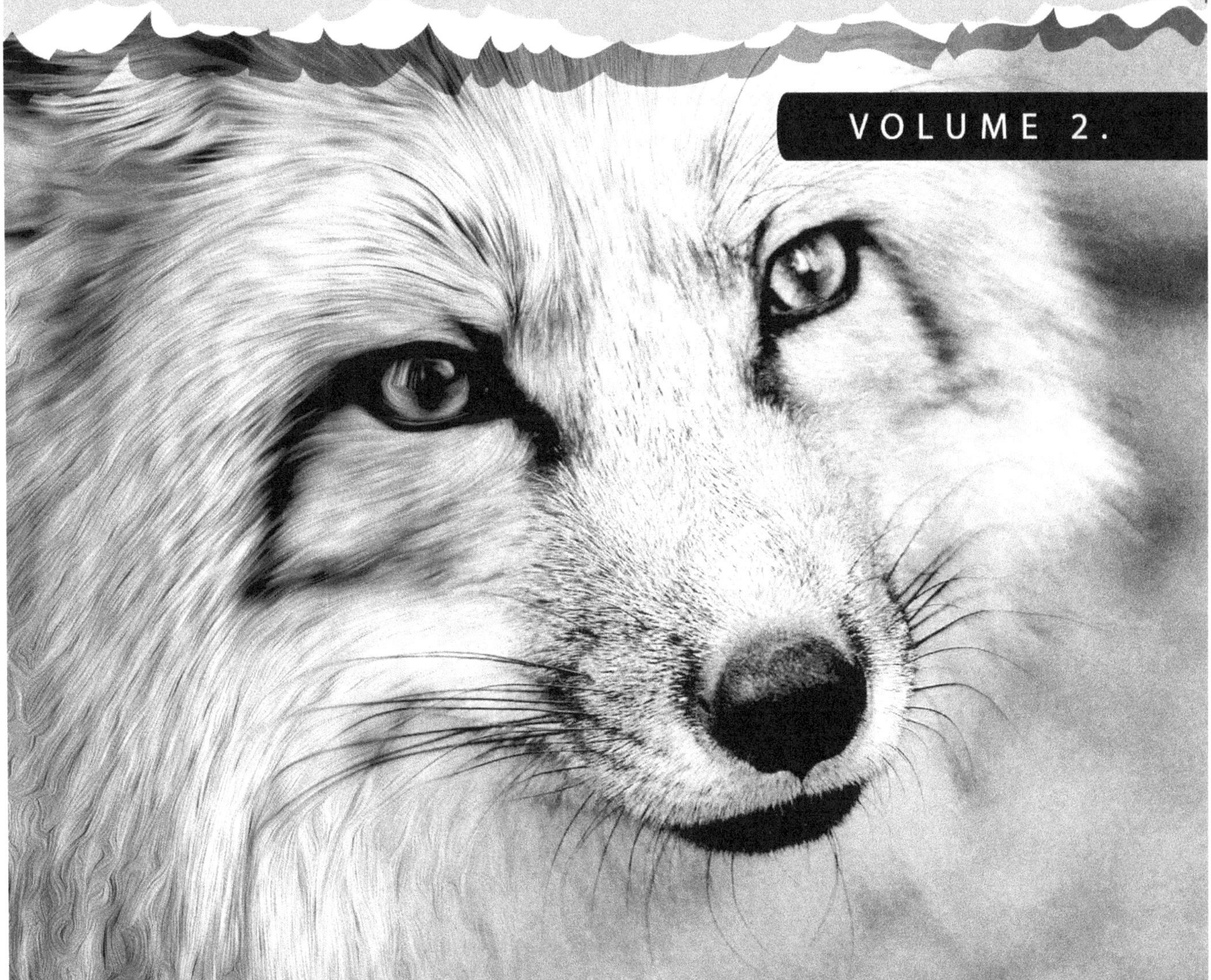

COLOR TEST PAGE

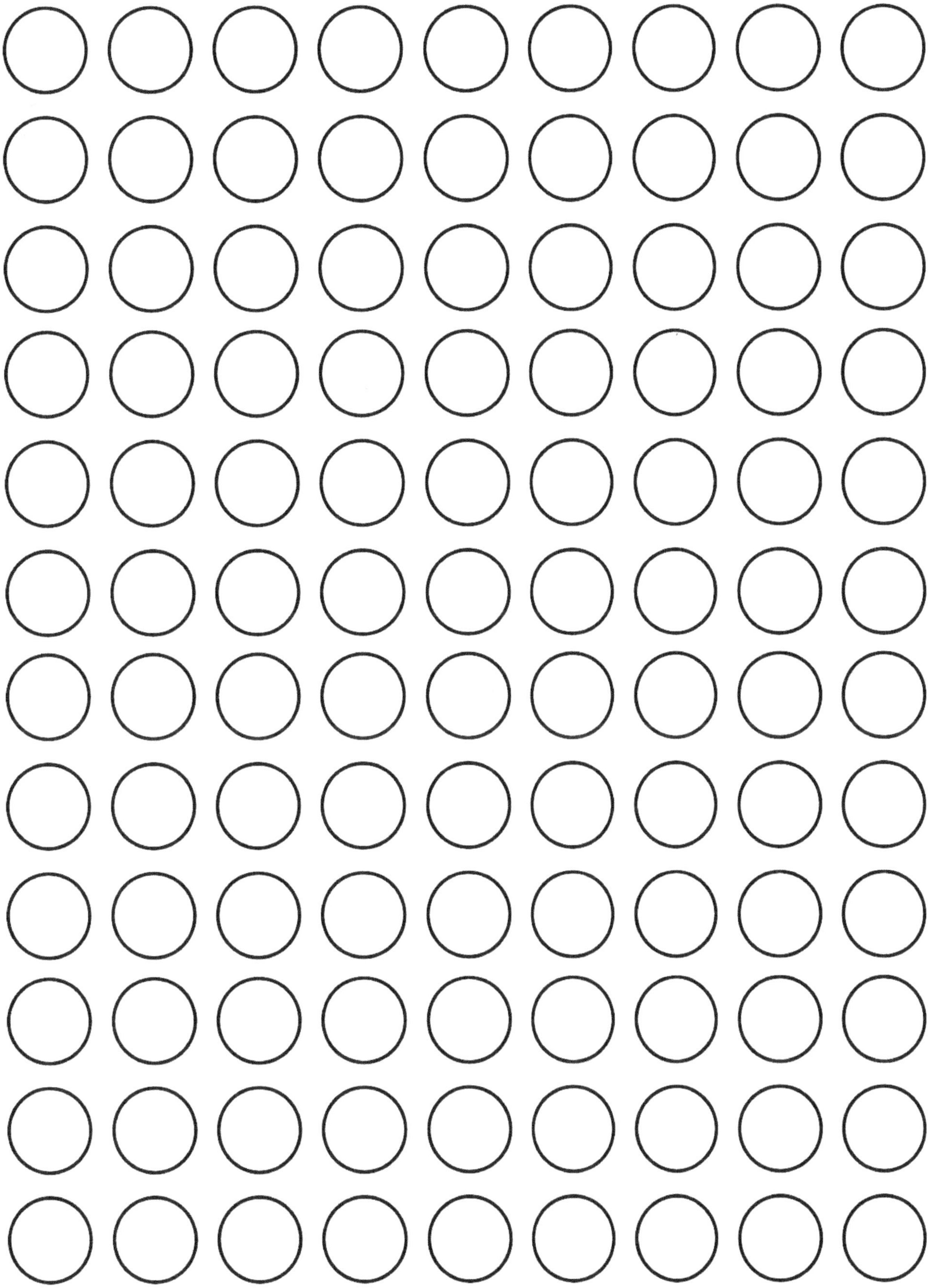

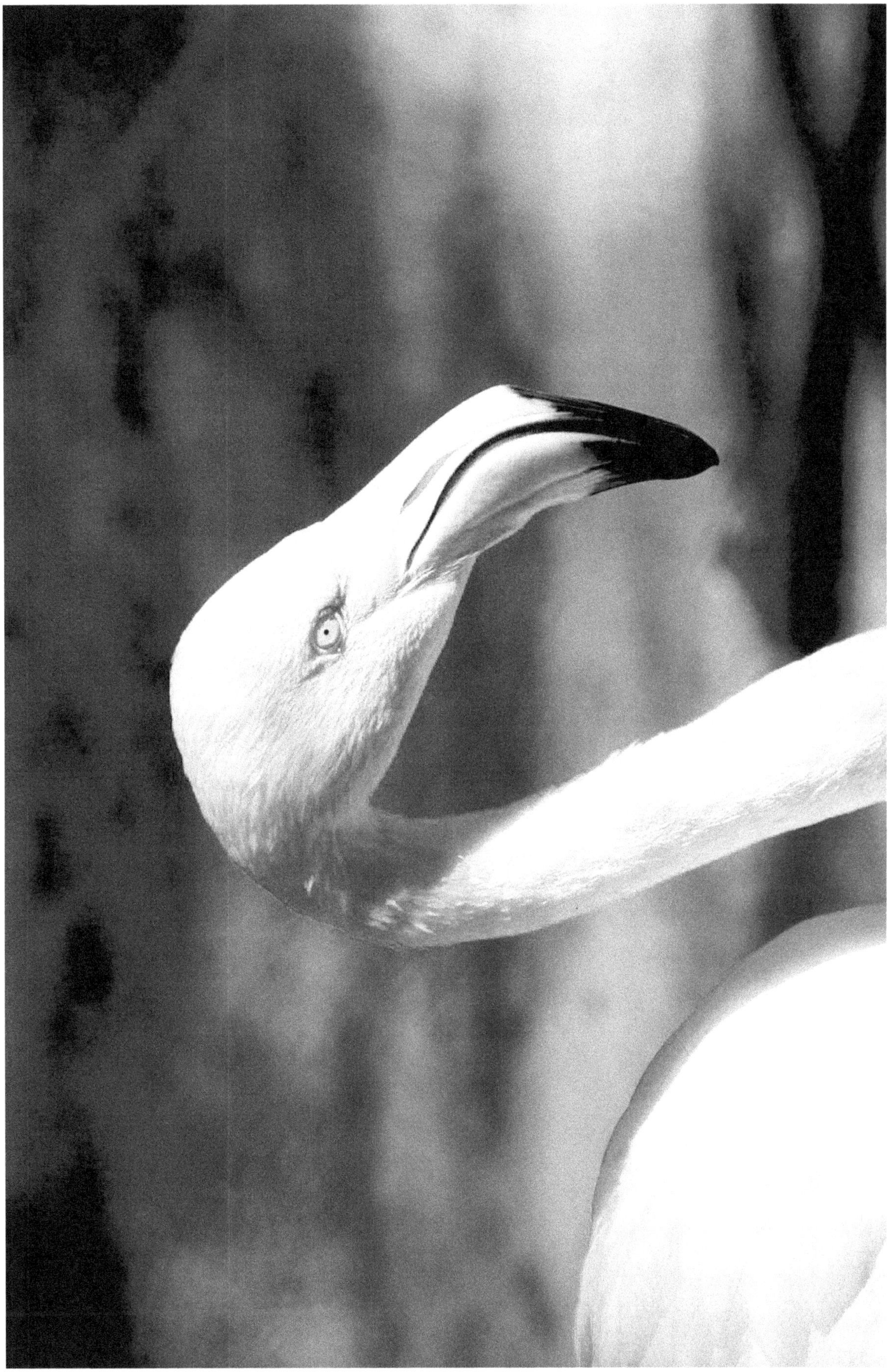

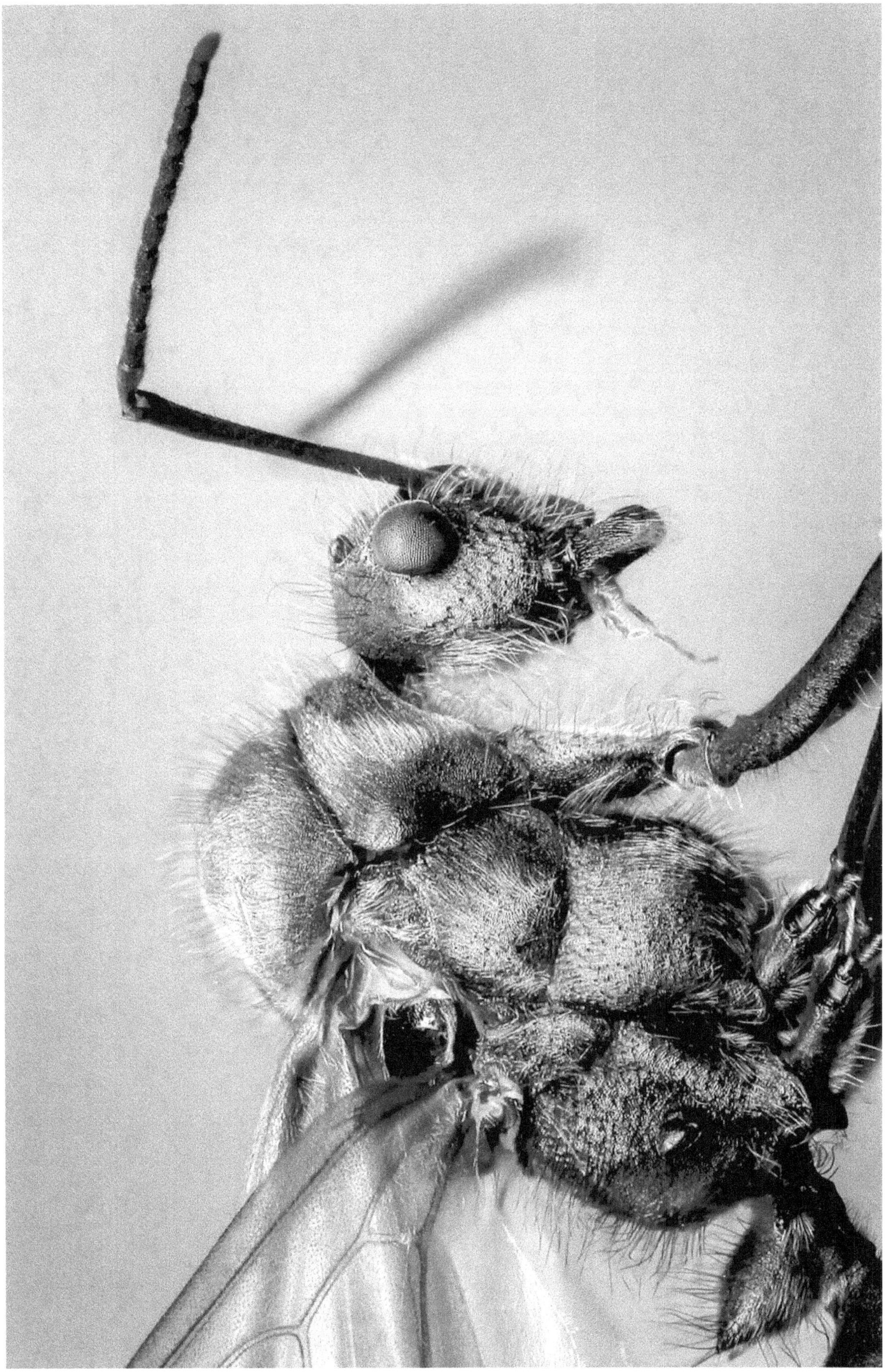

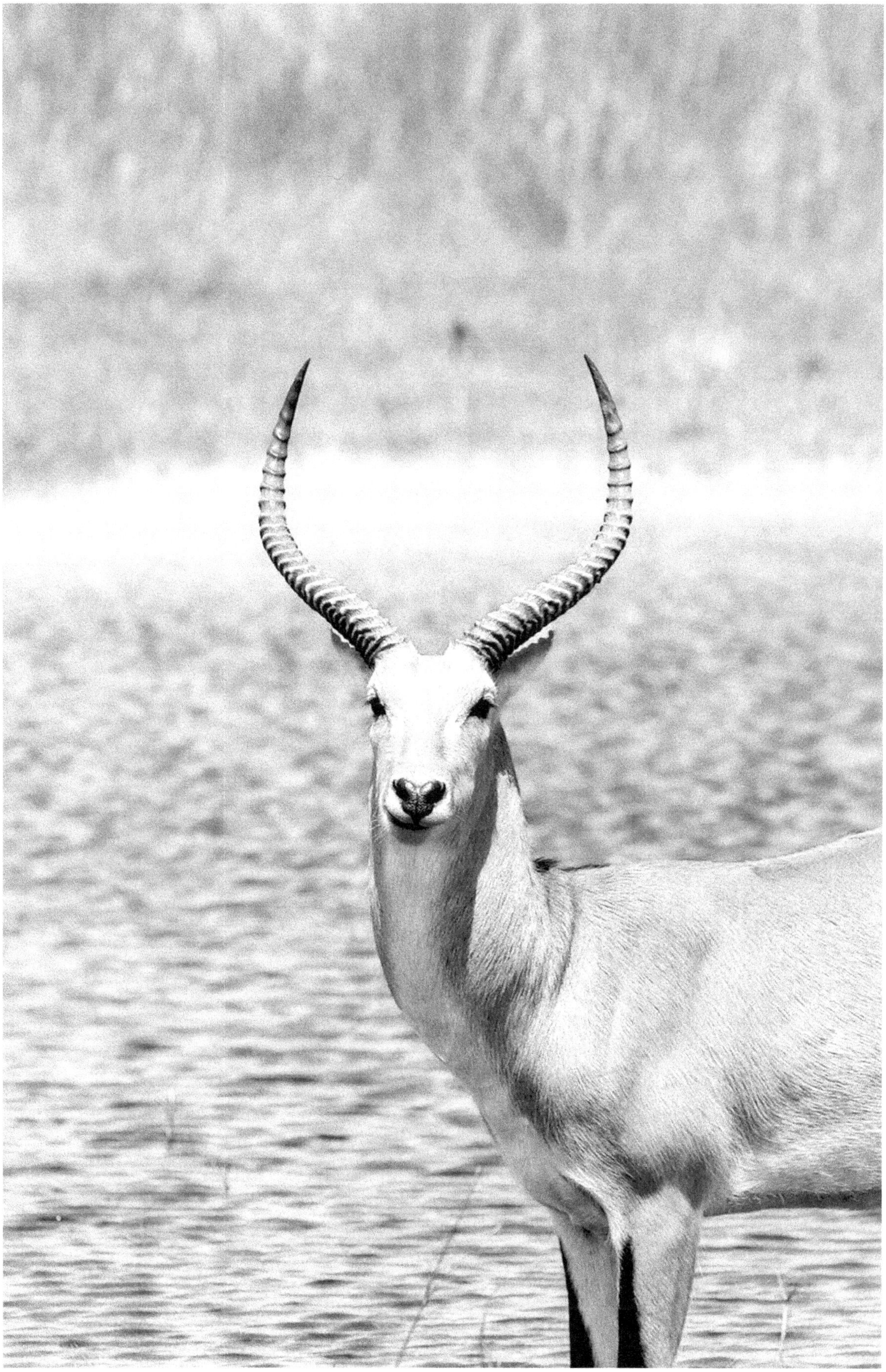

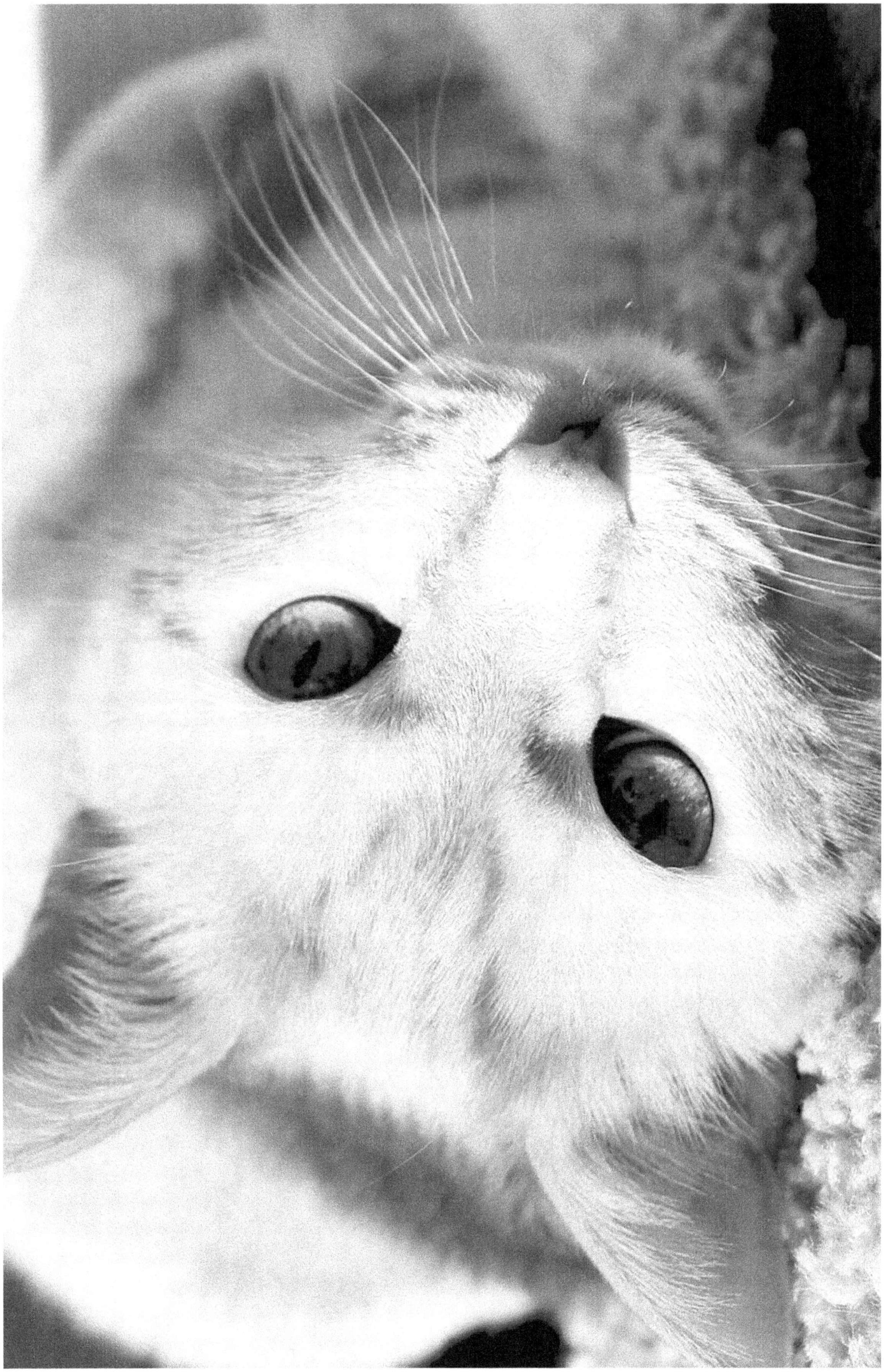

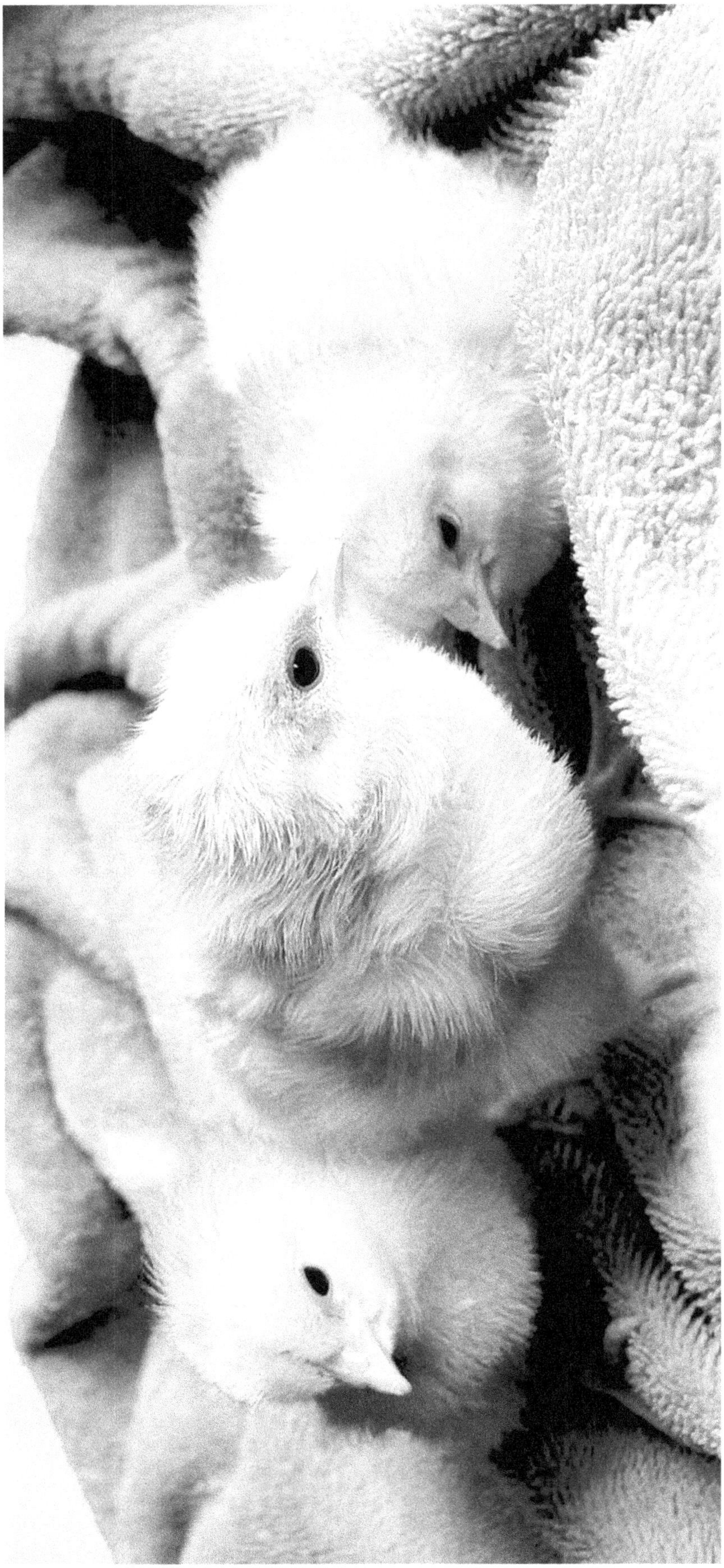

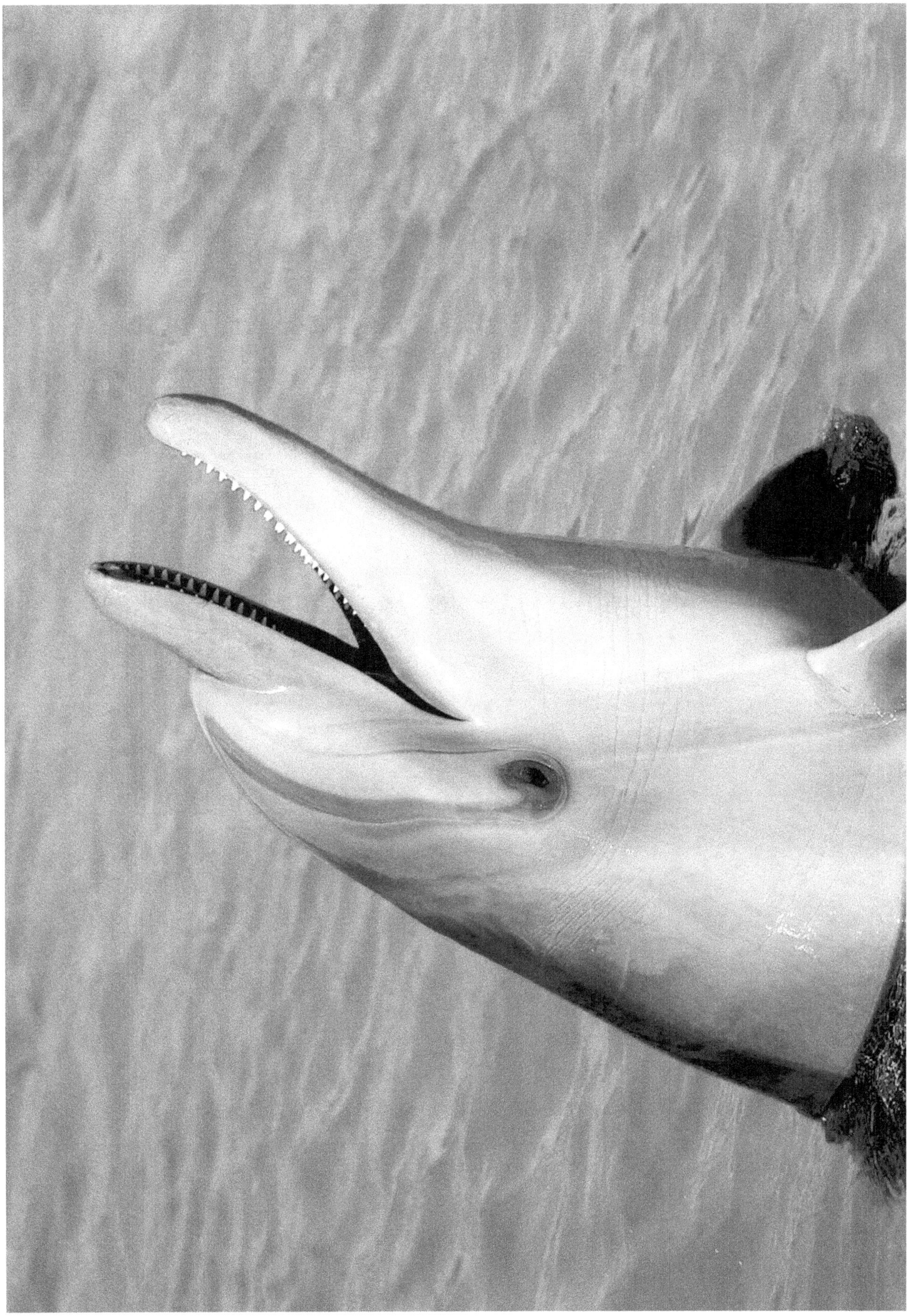

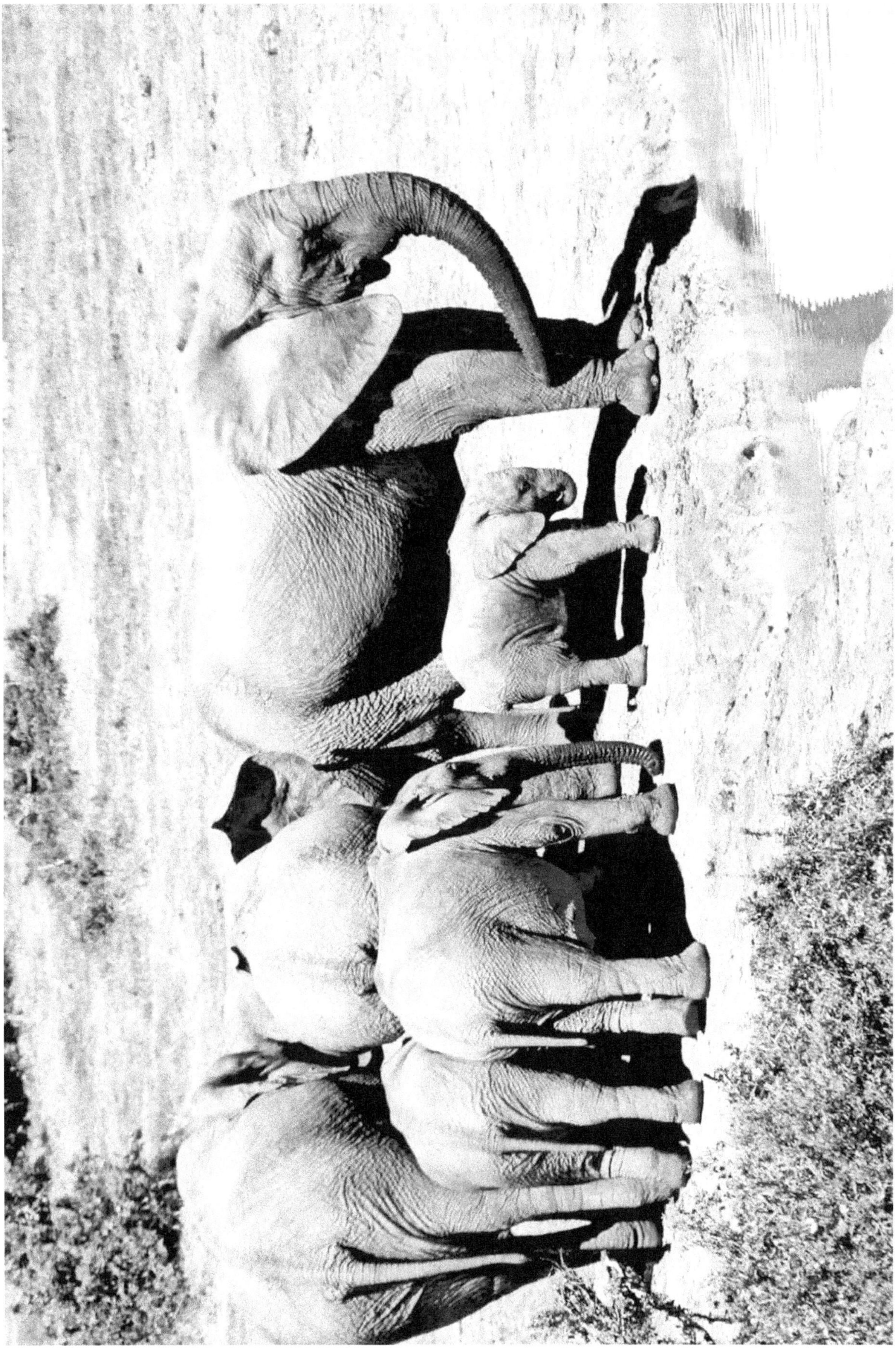

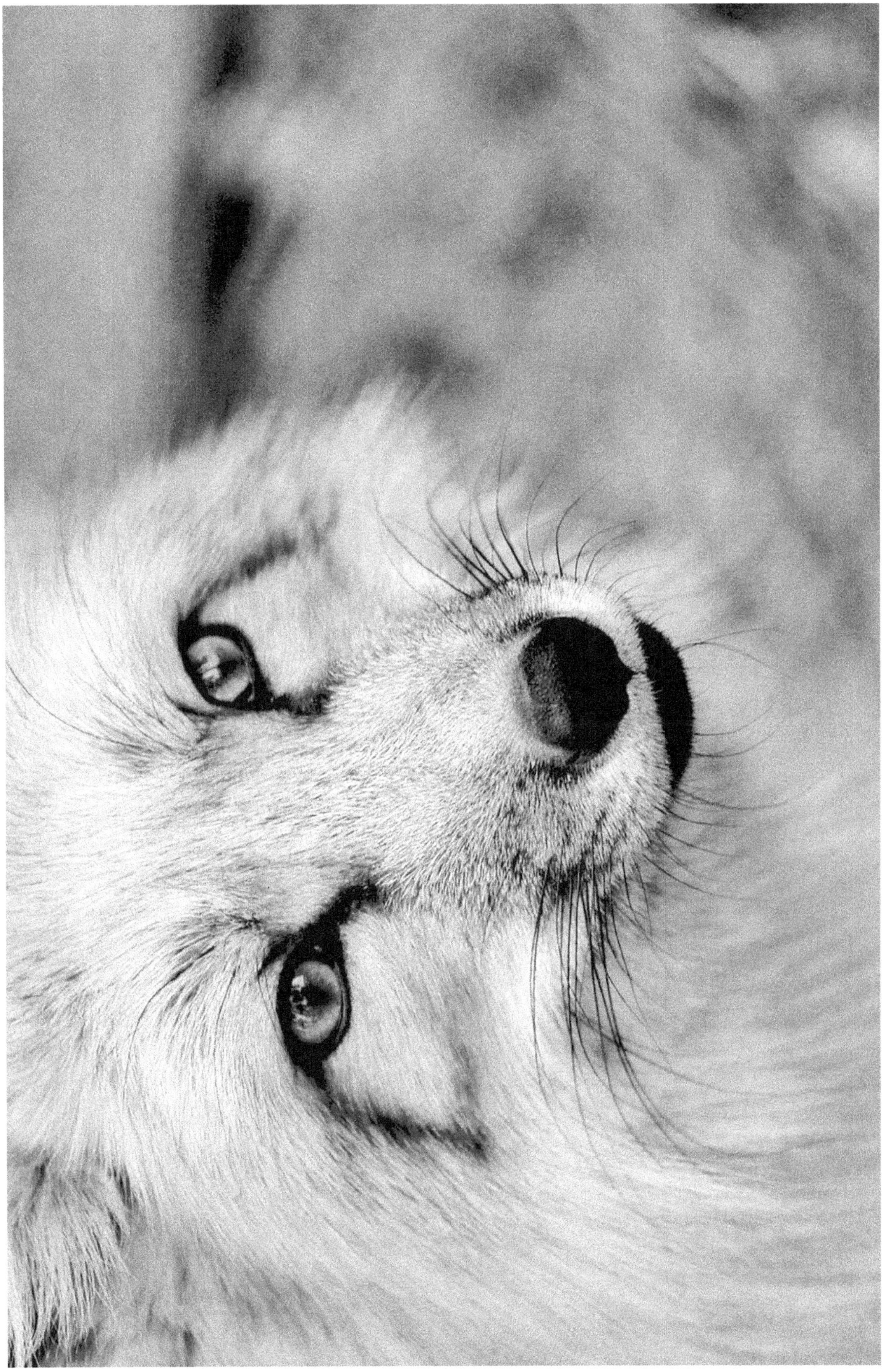

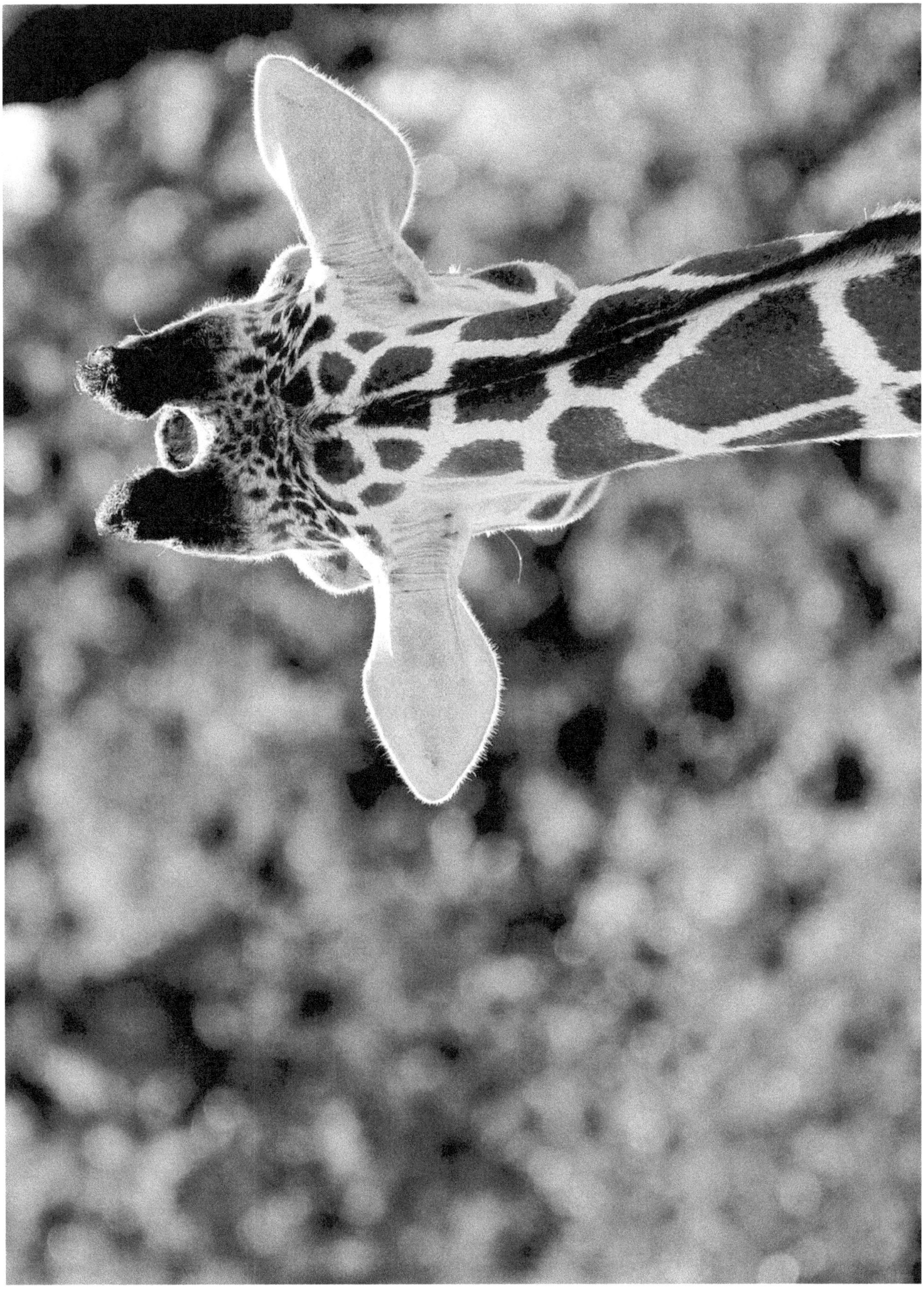

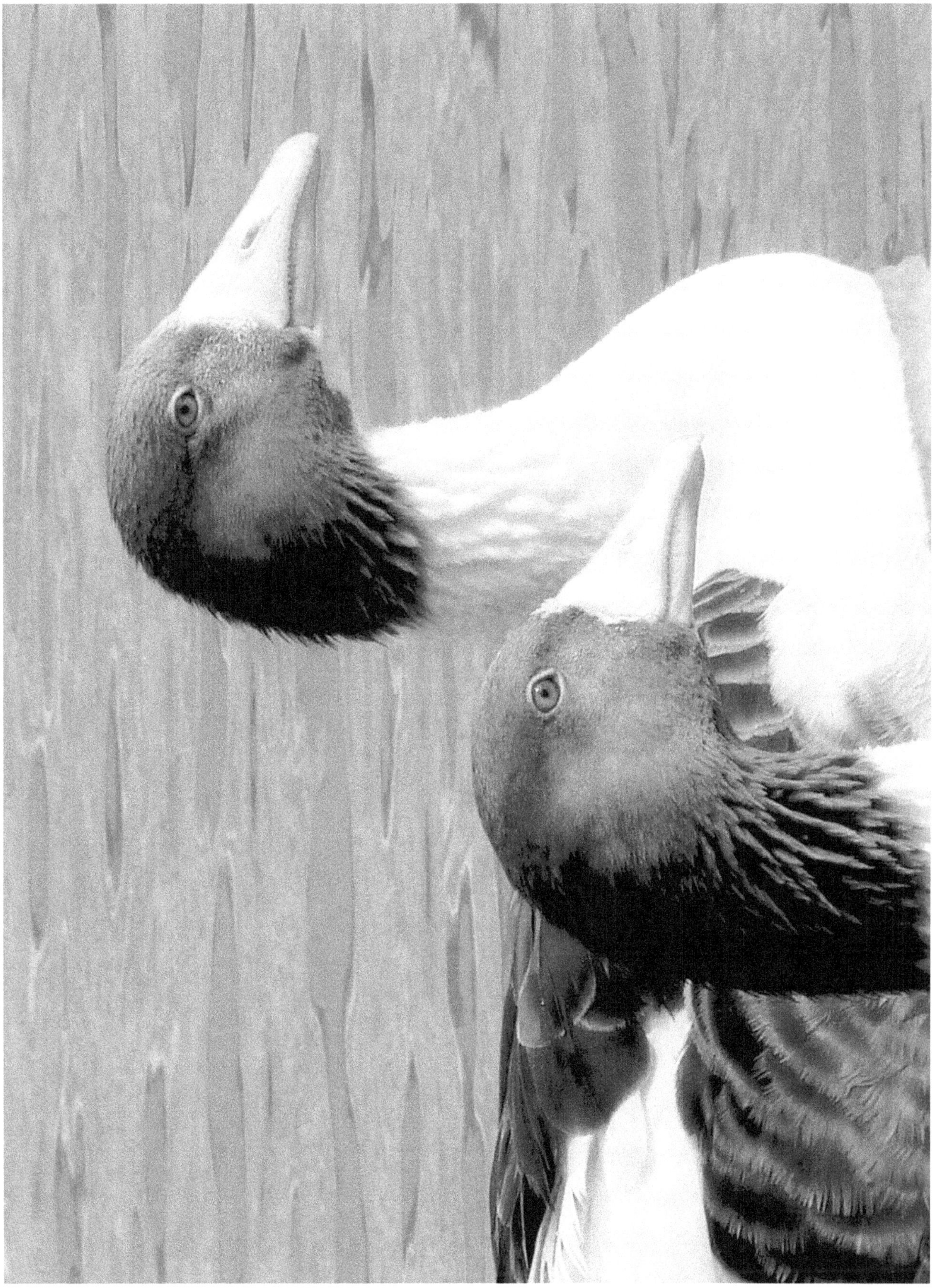

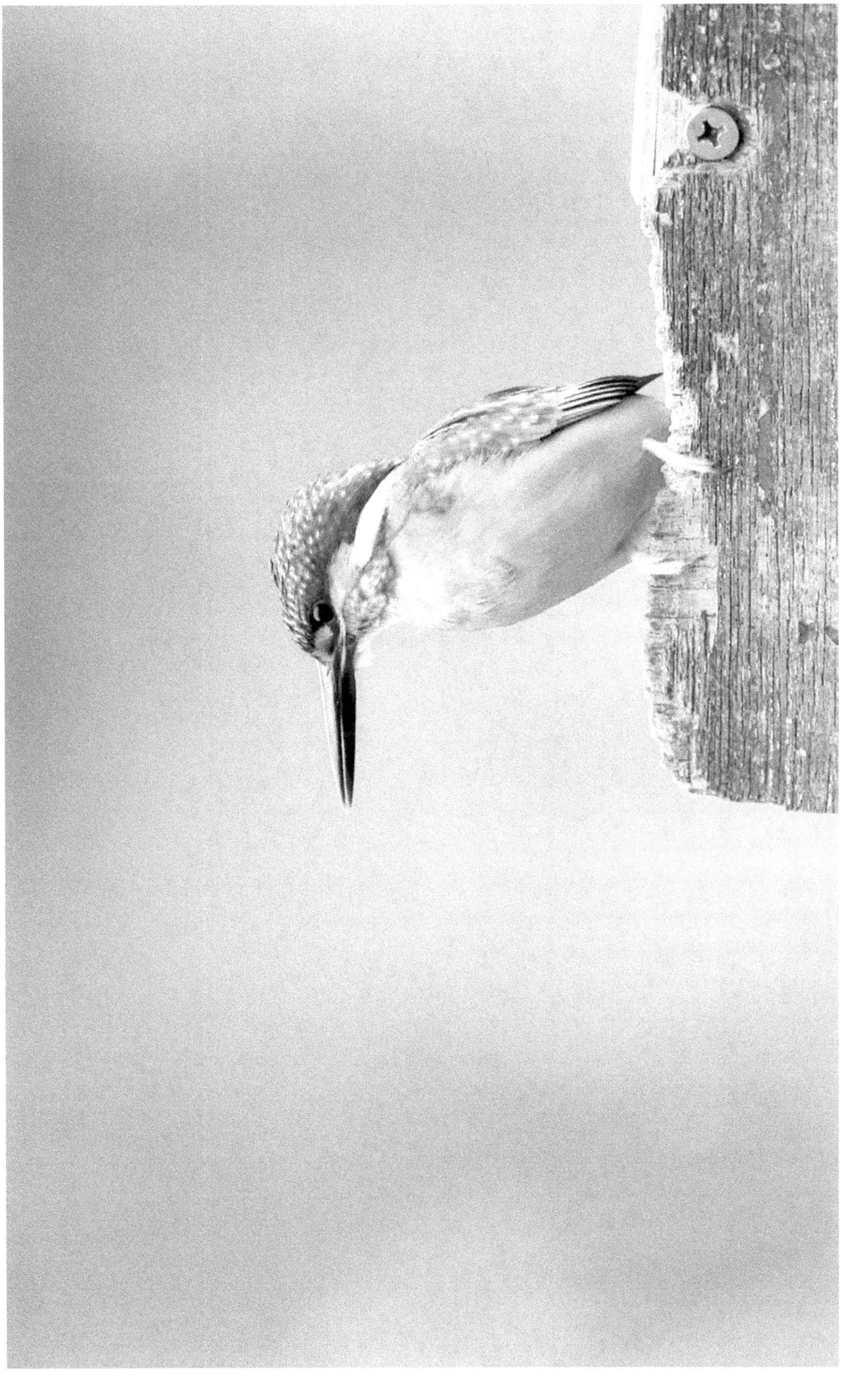

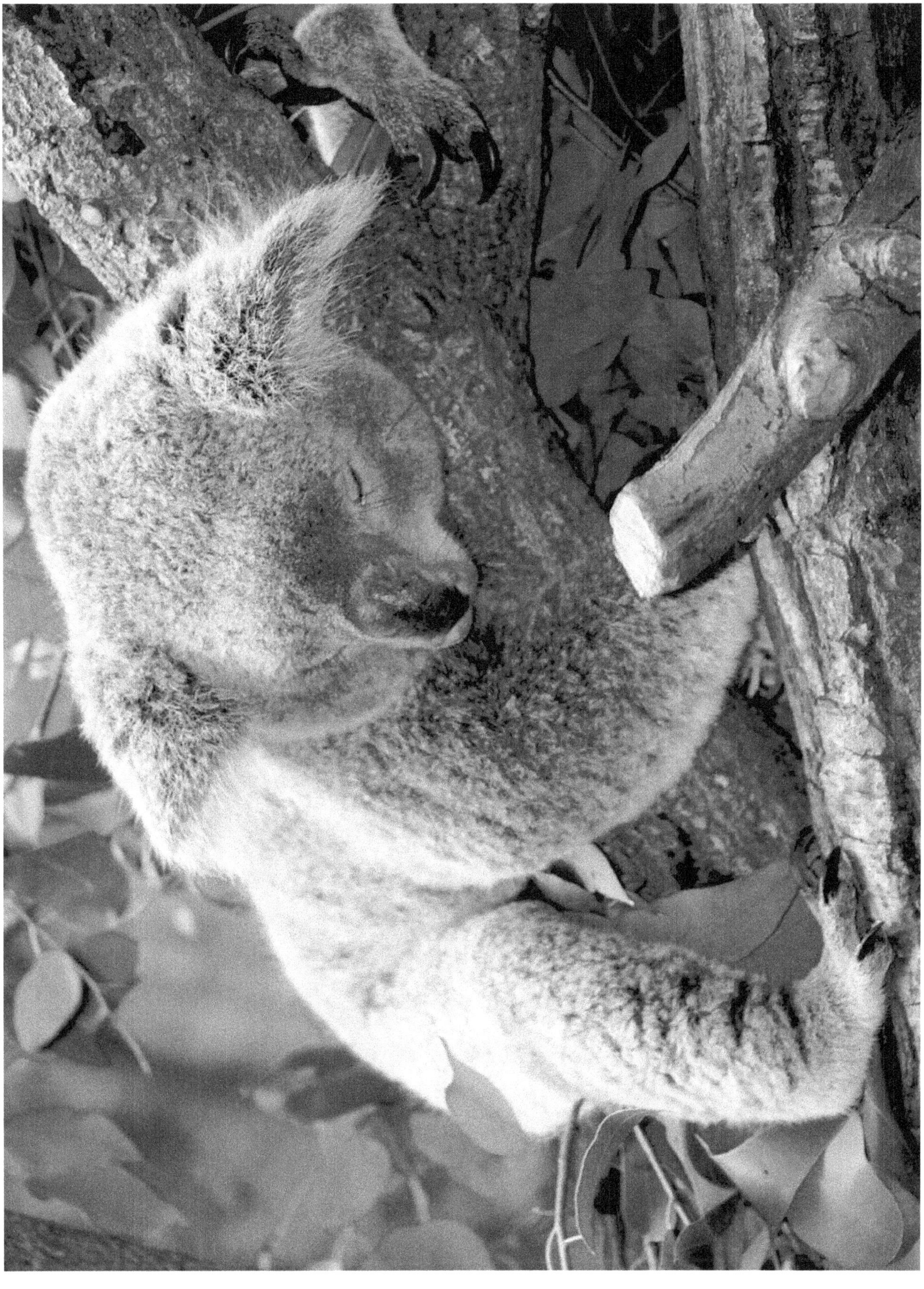

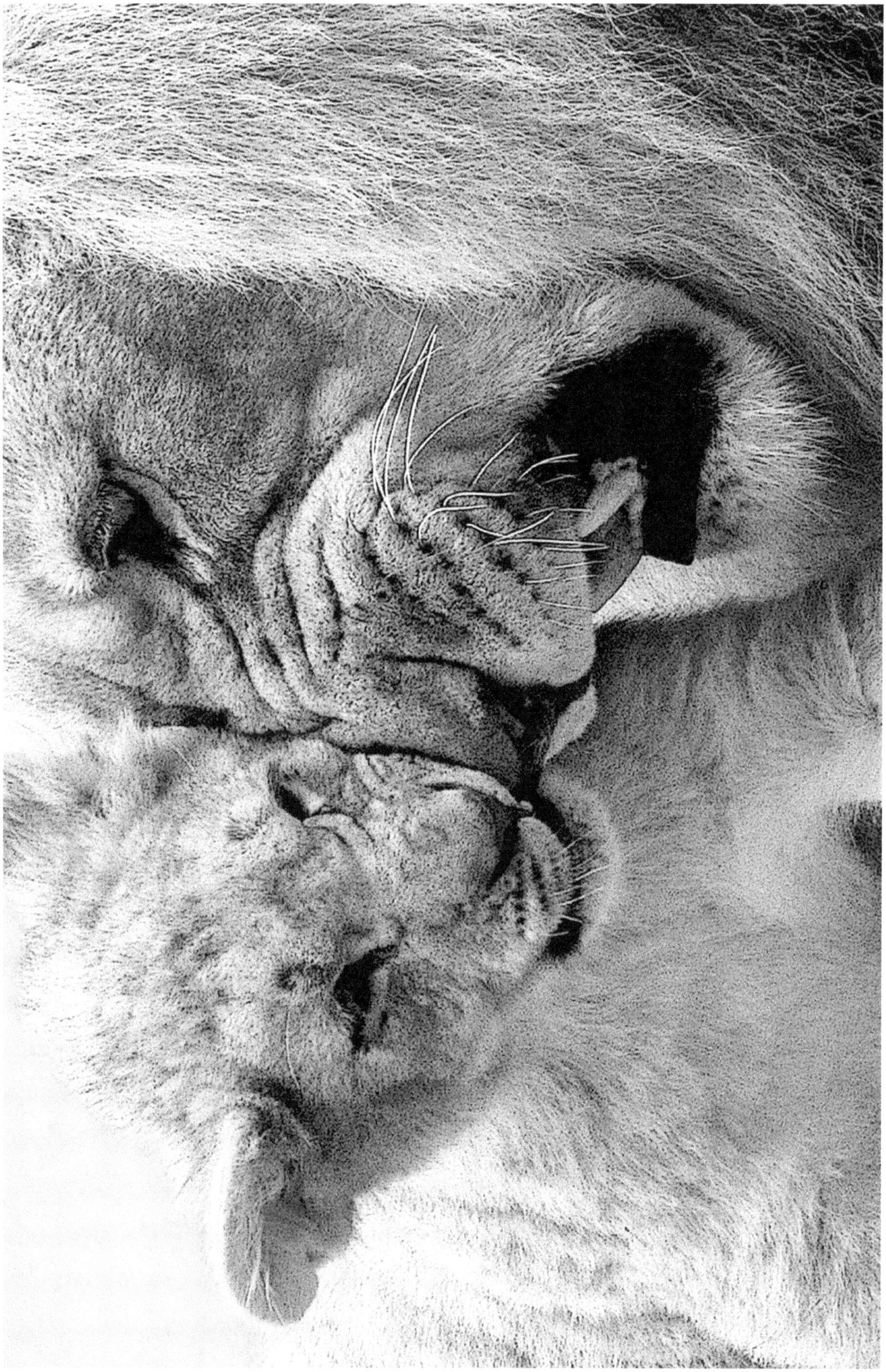

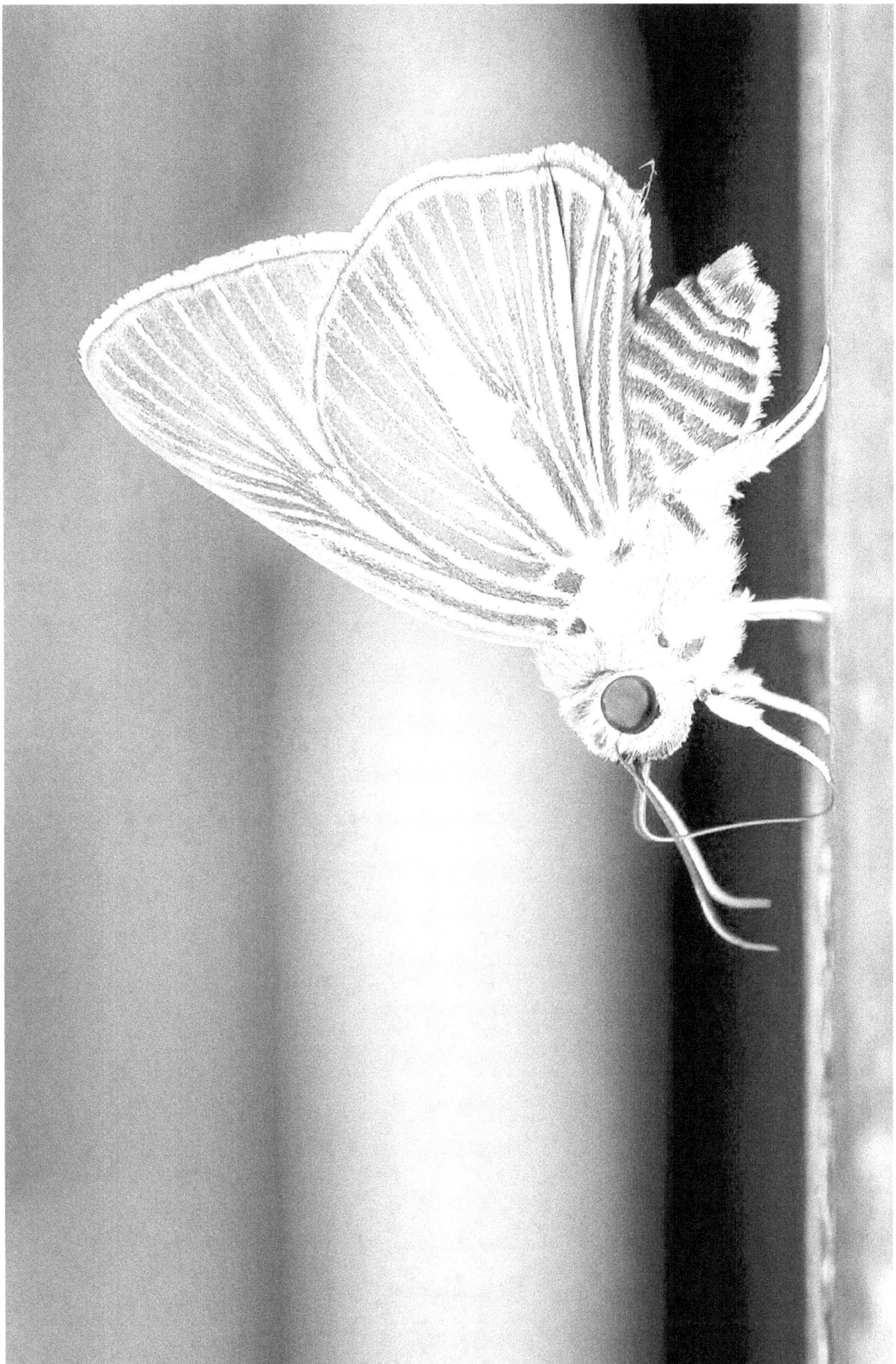

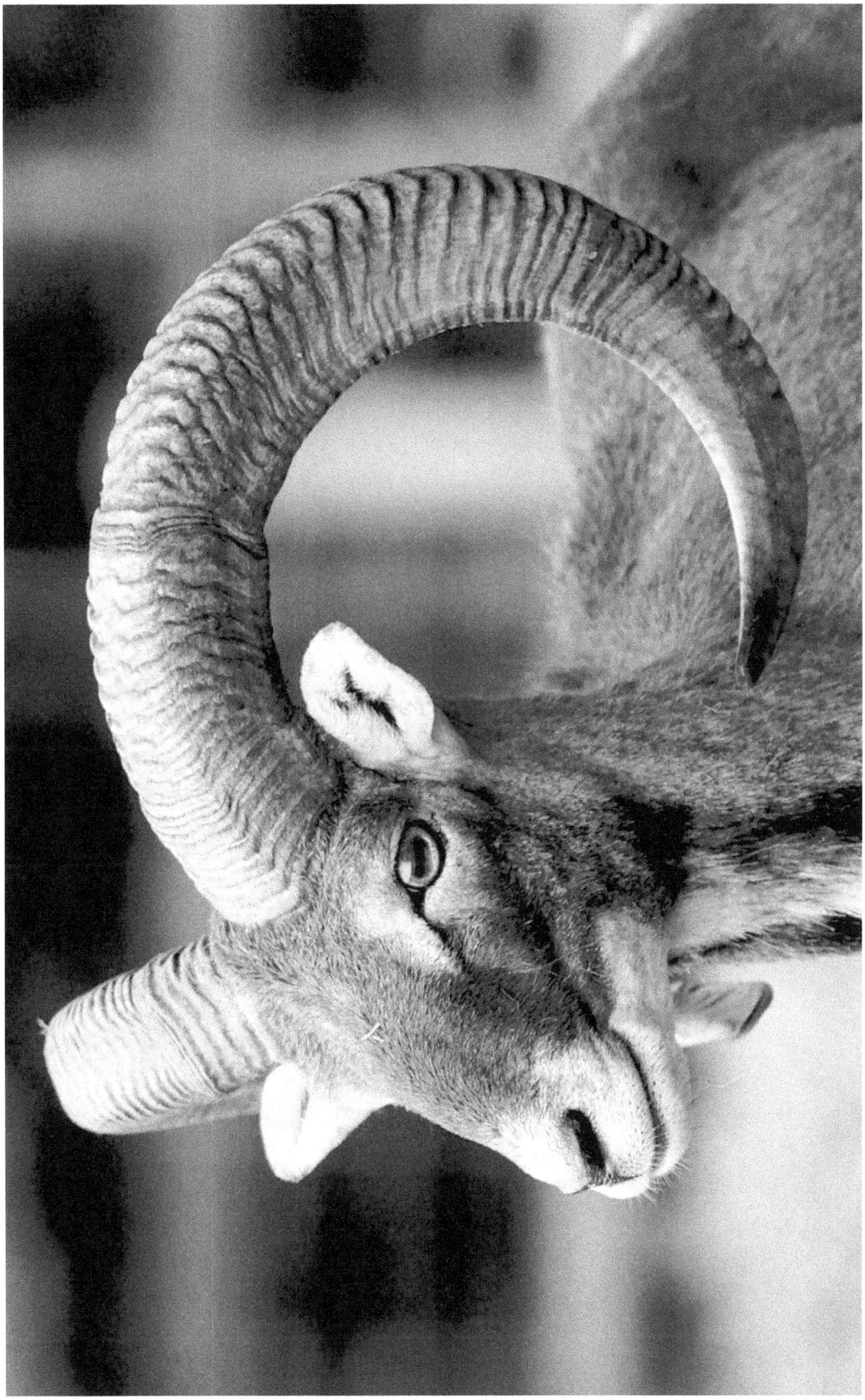

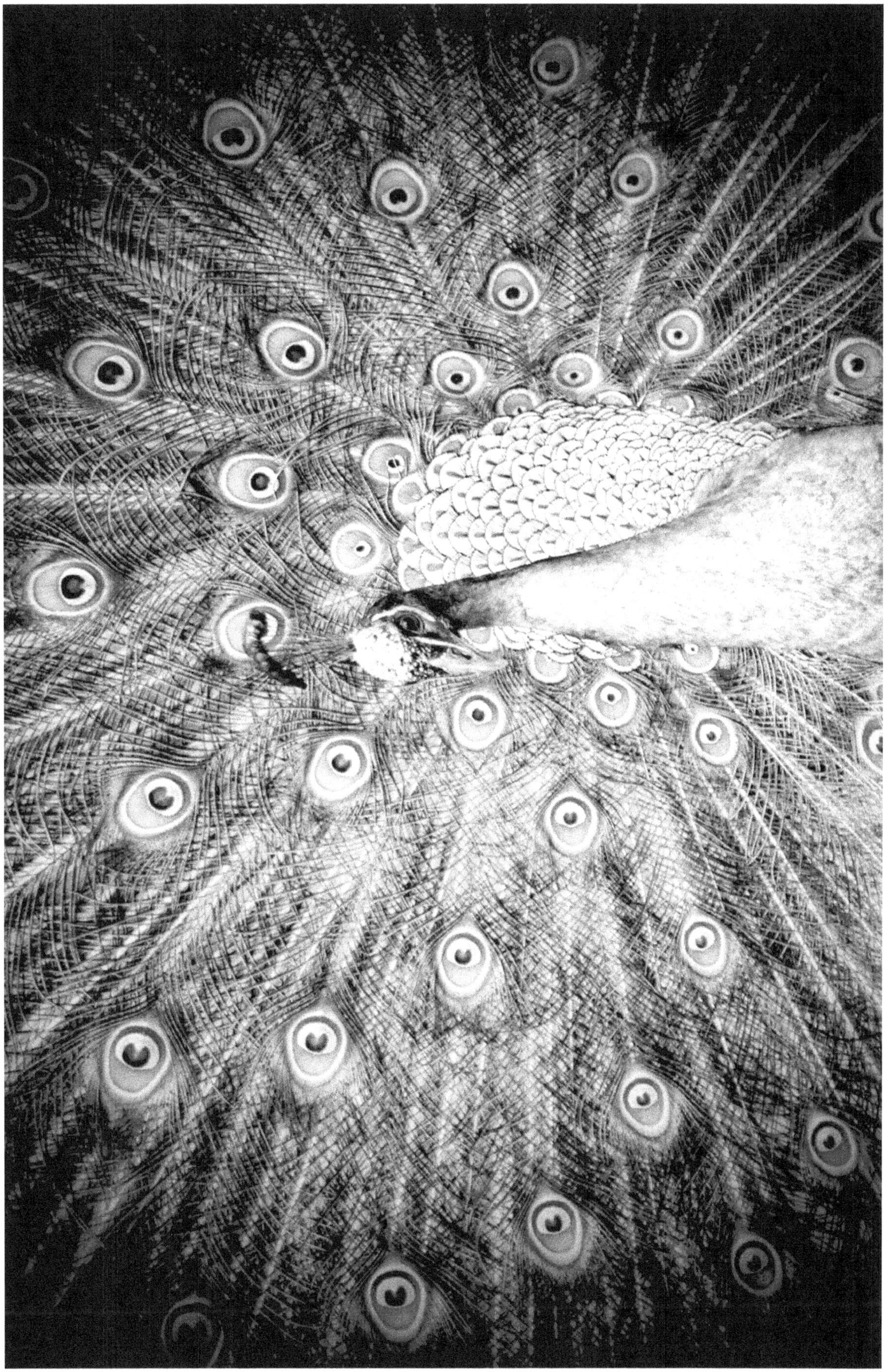

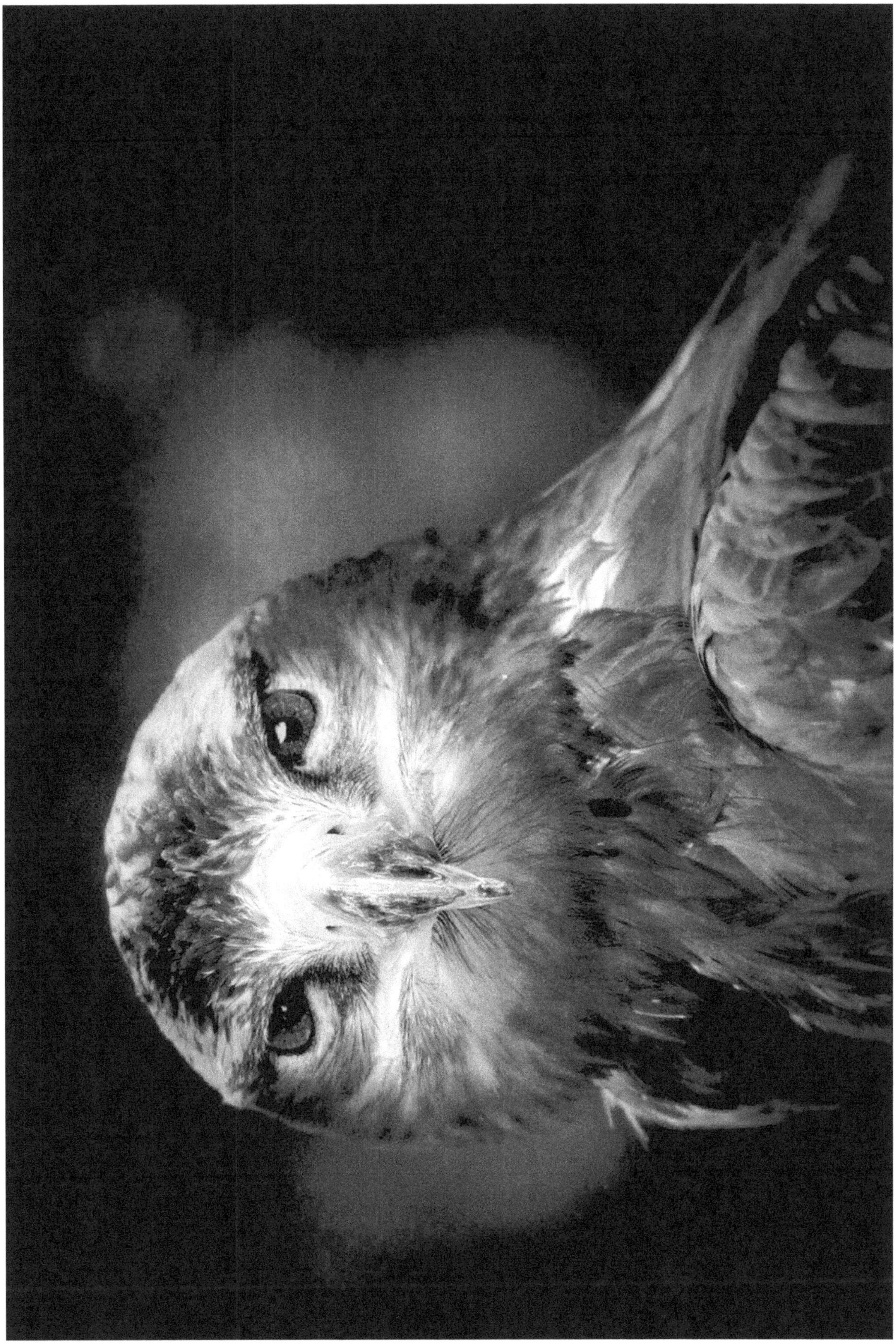

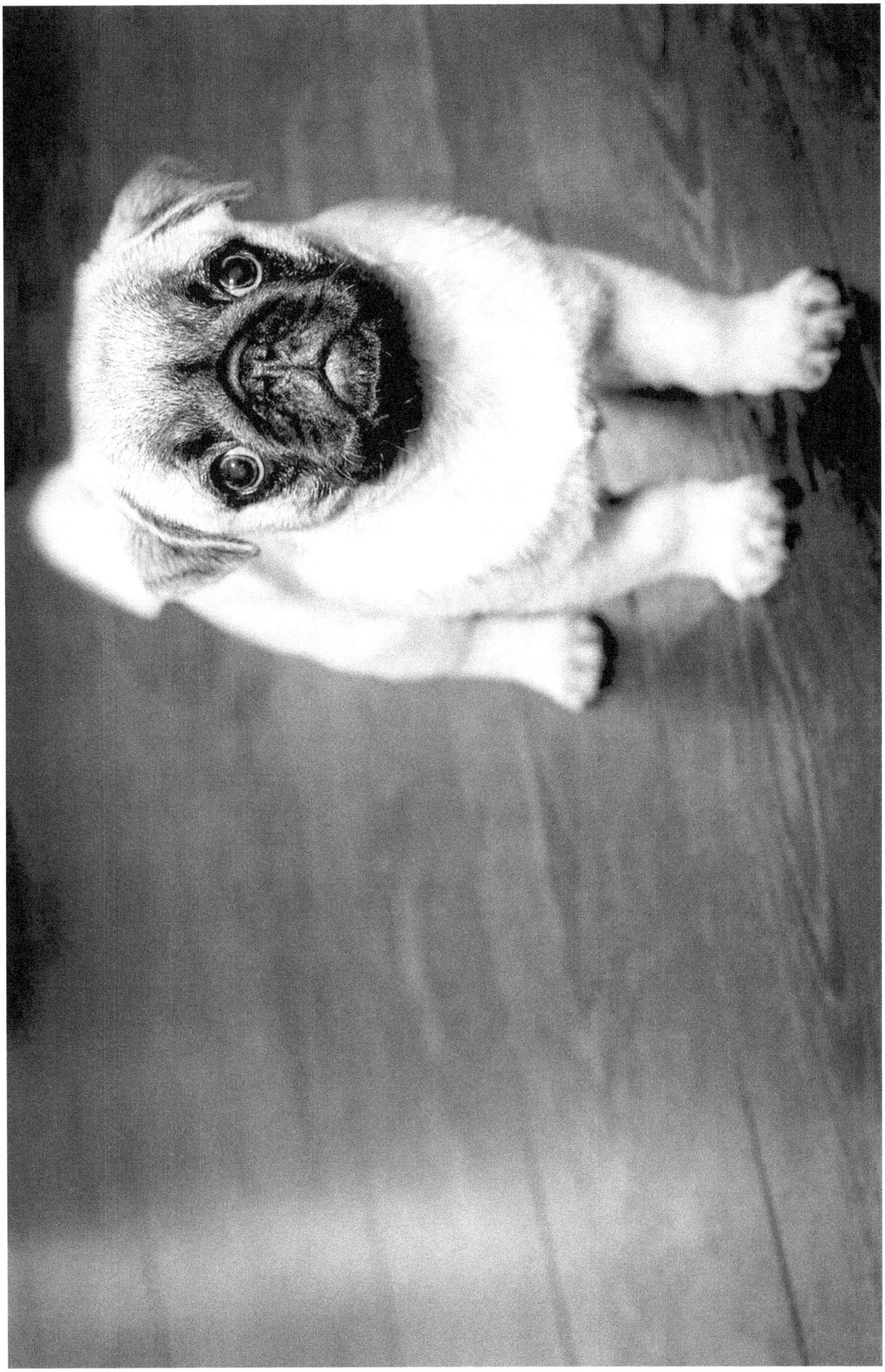

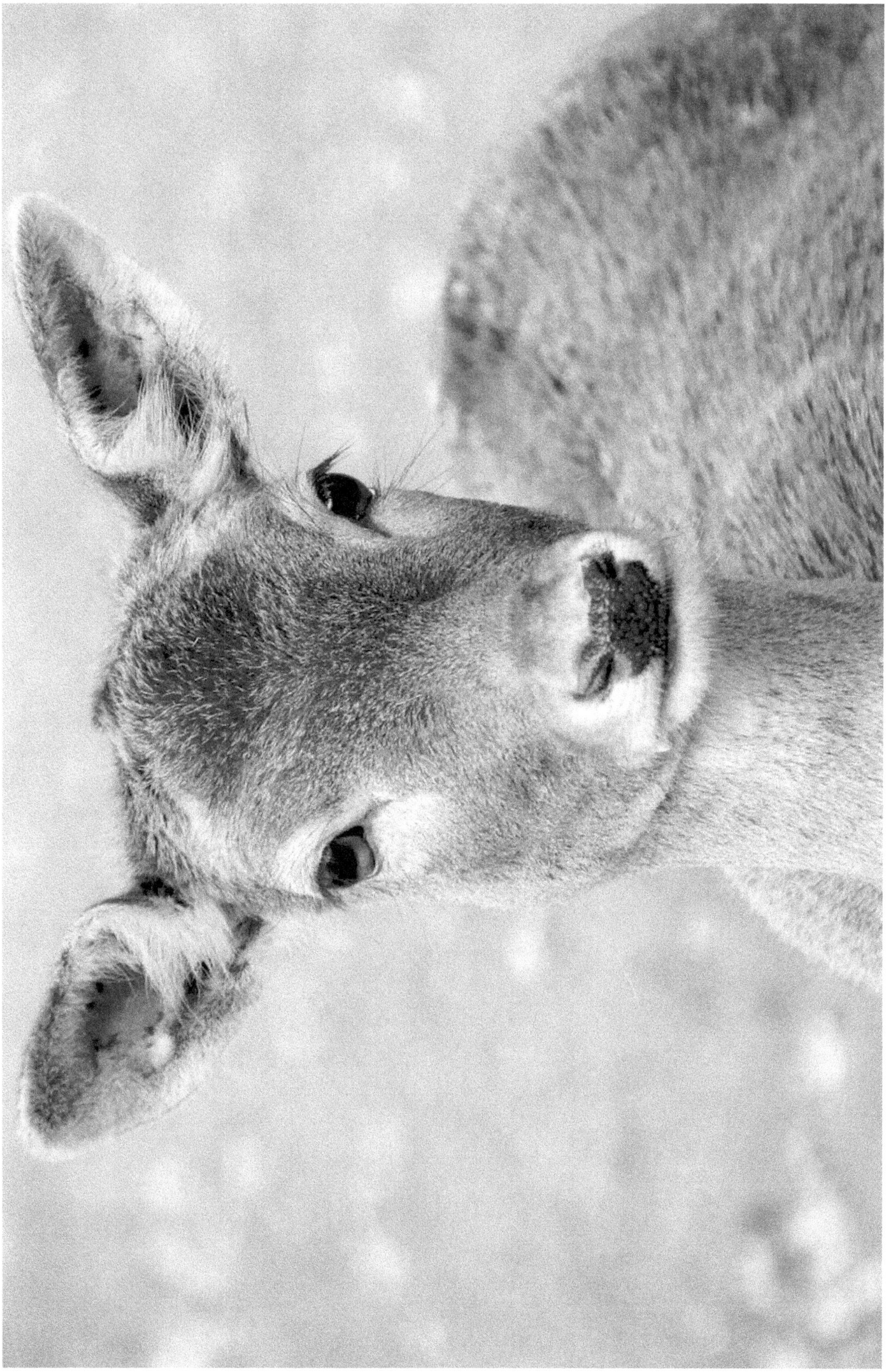

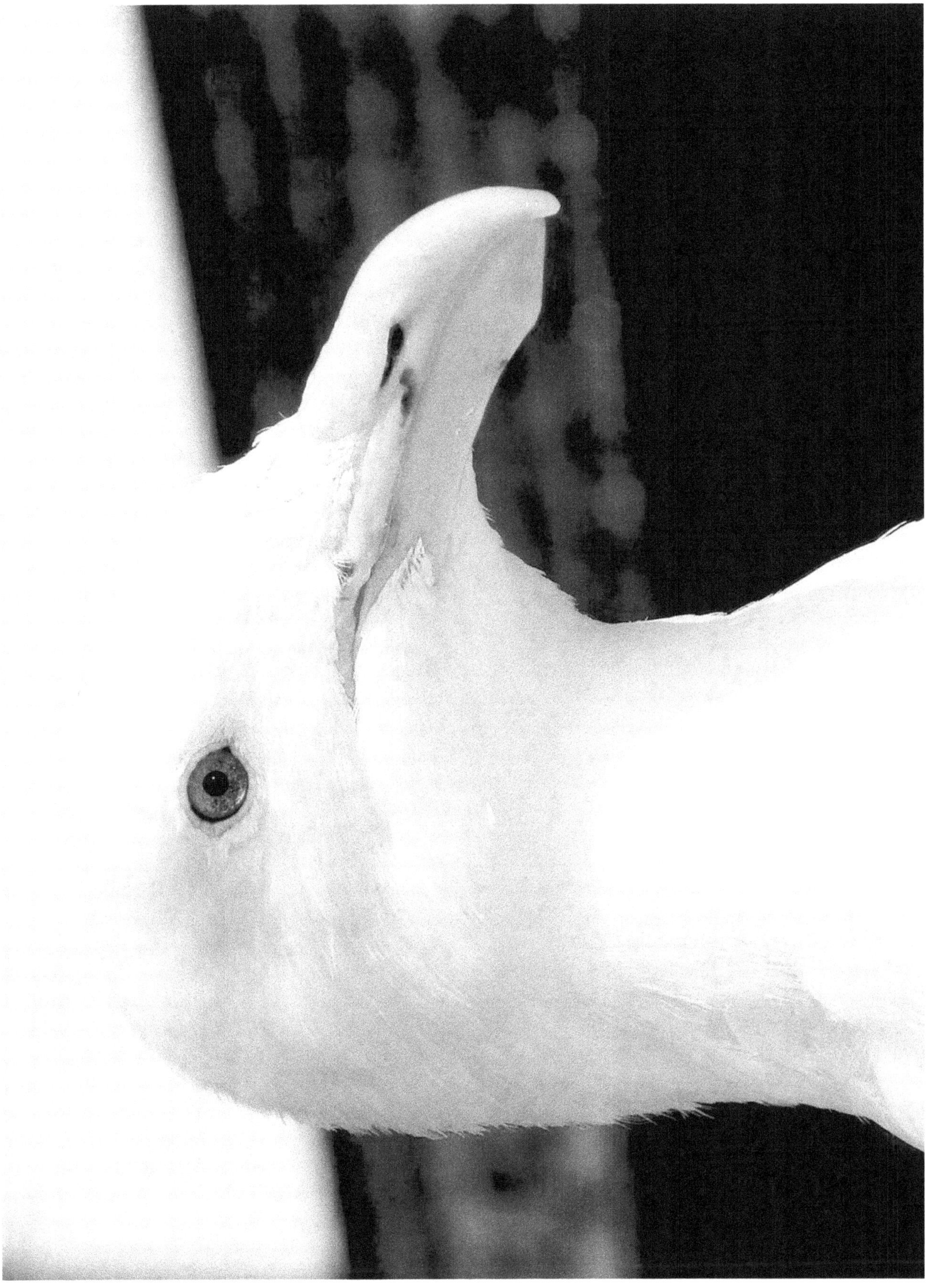

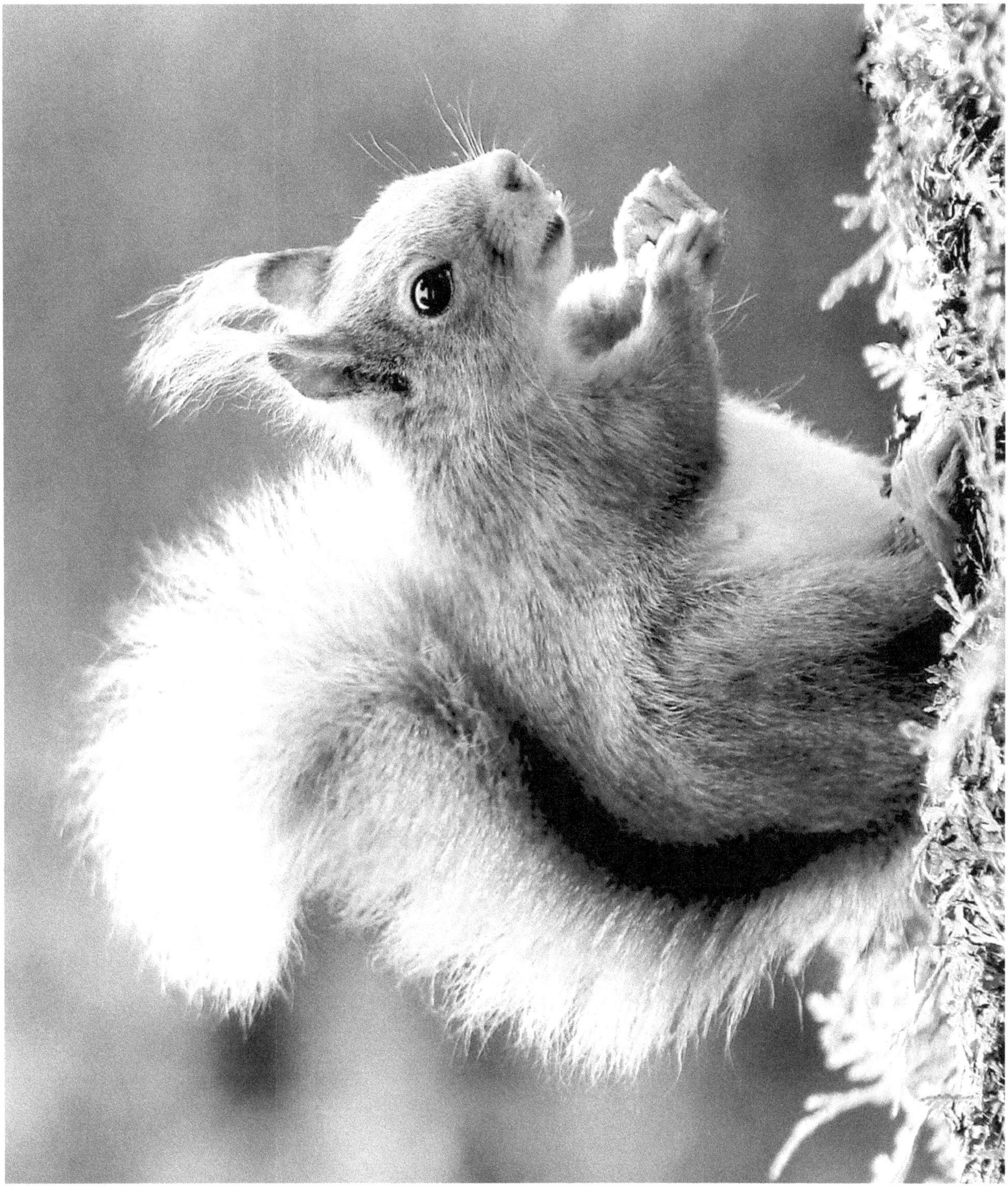

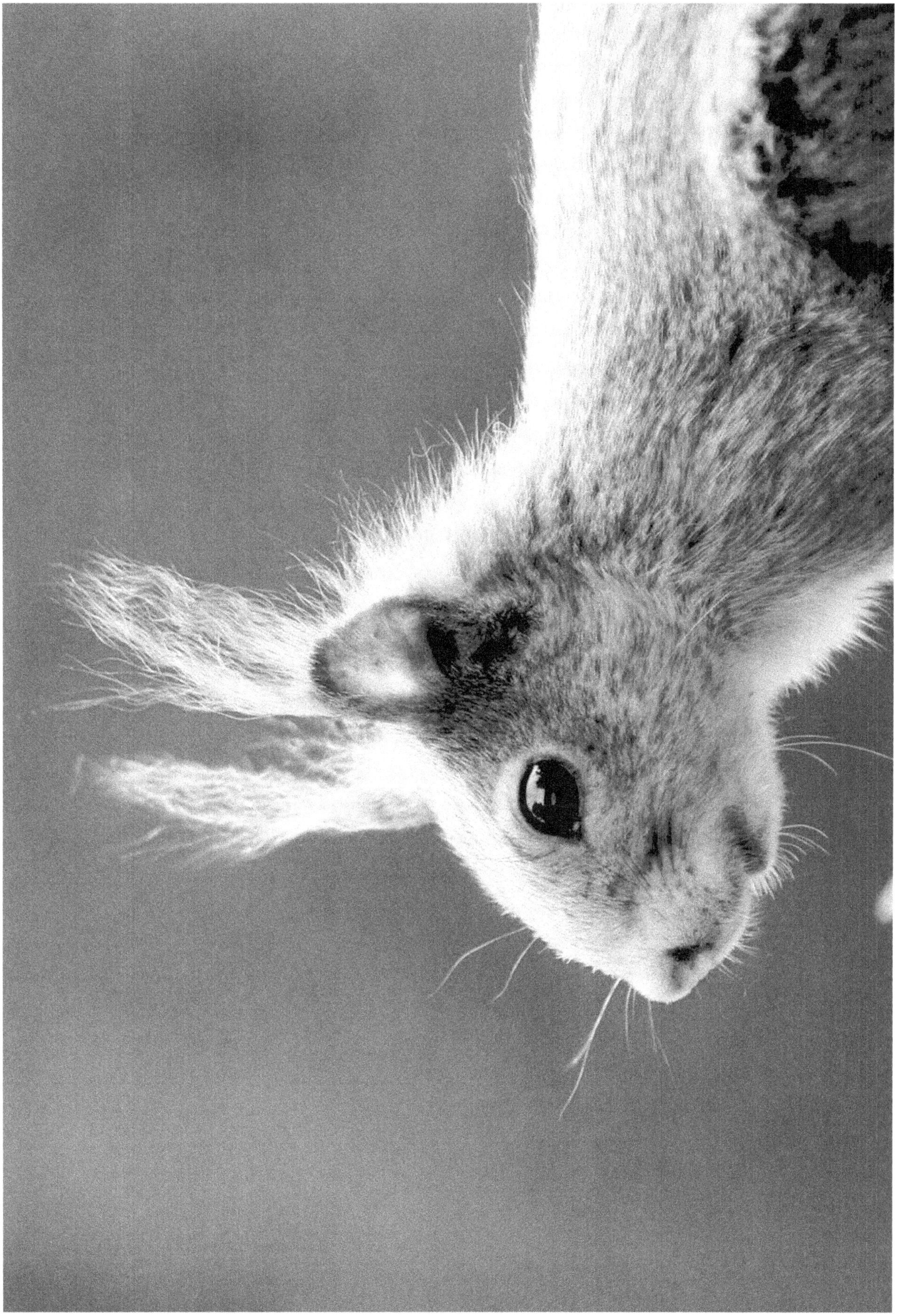

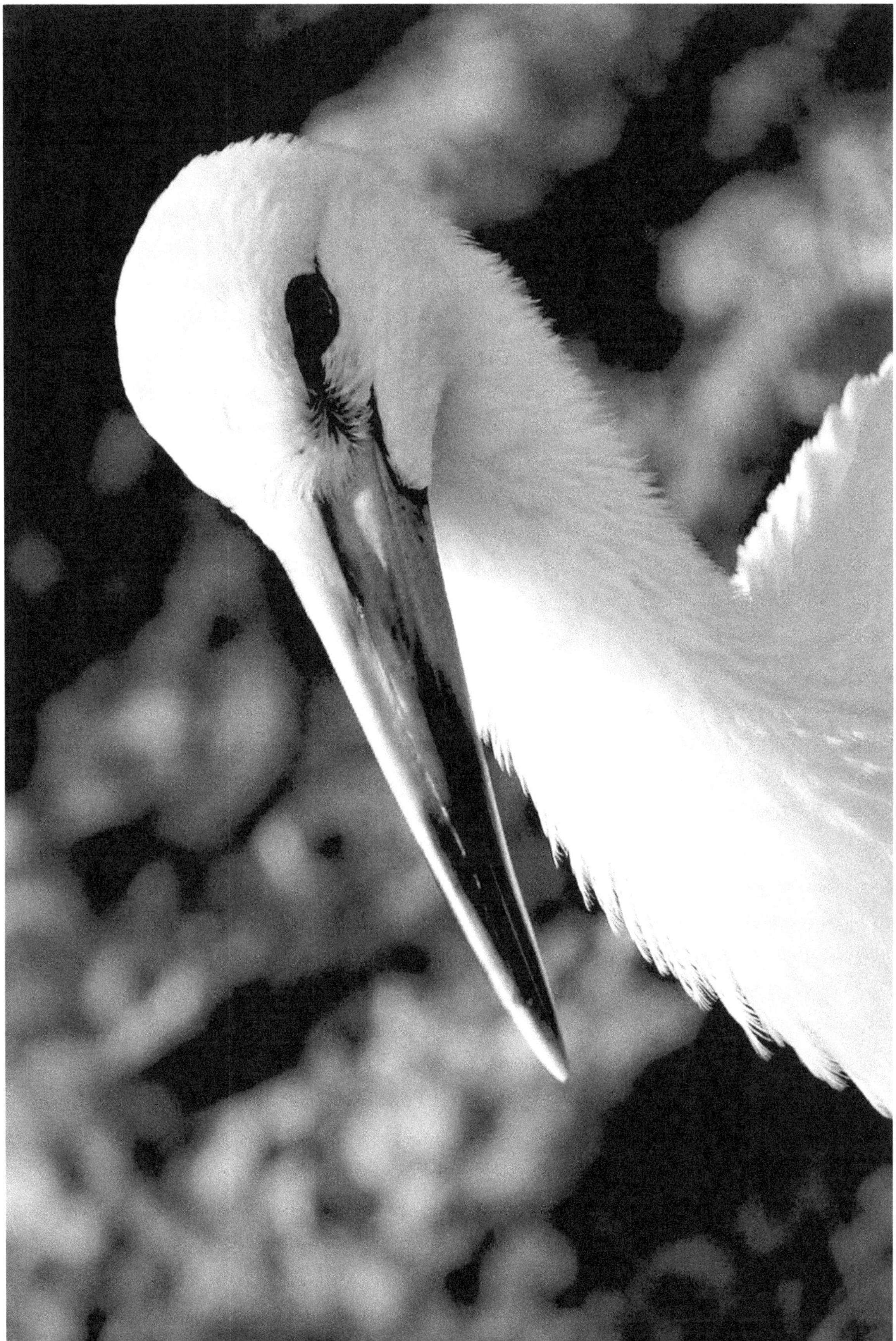

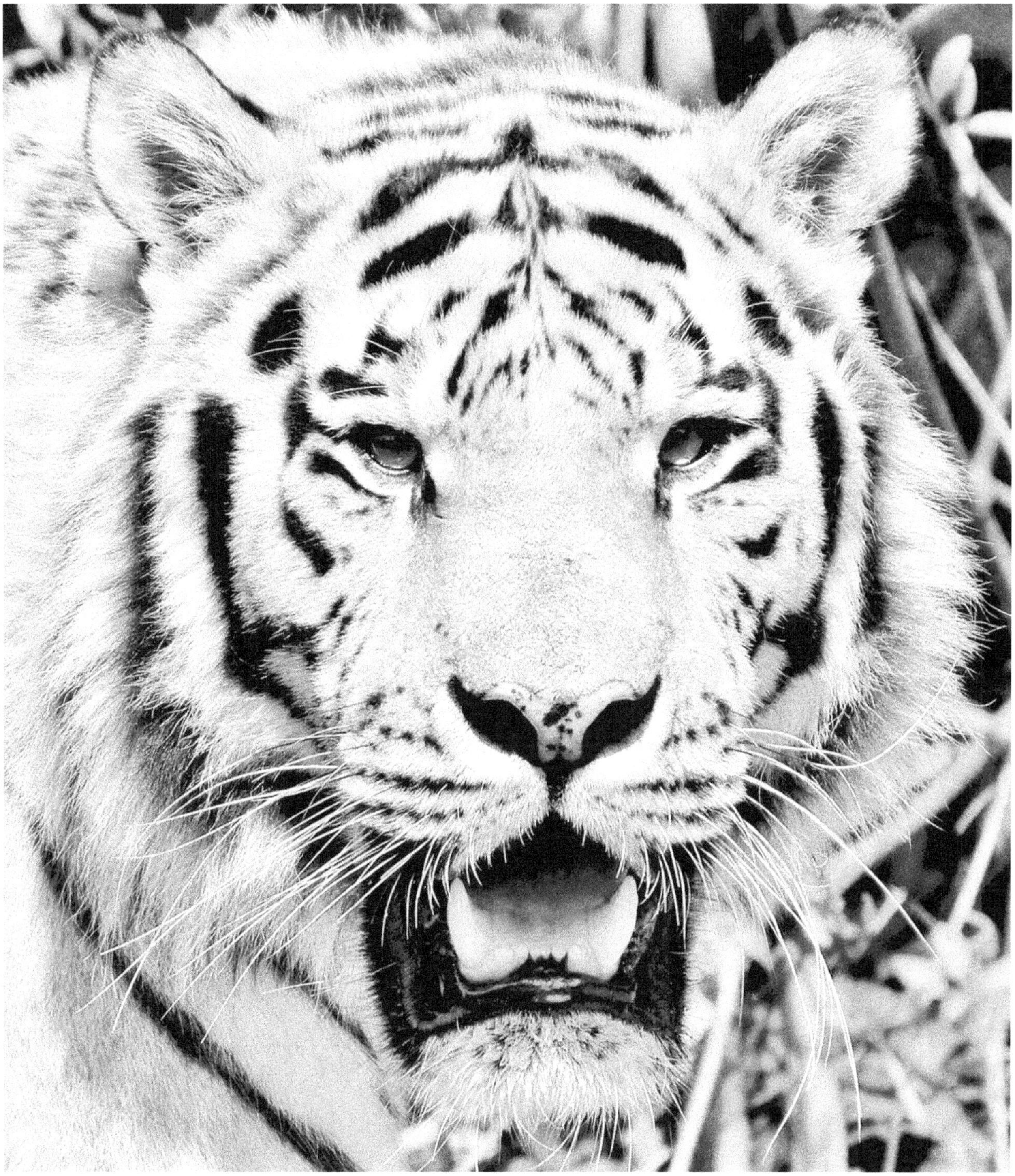

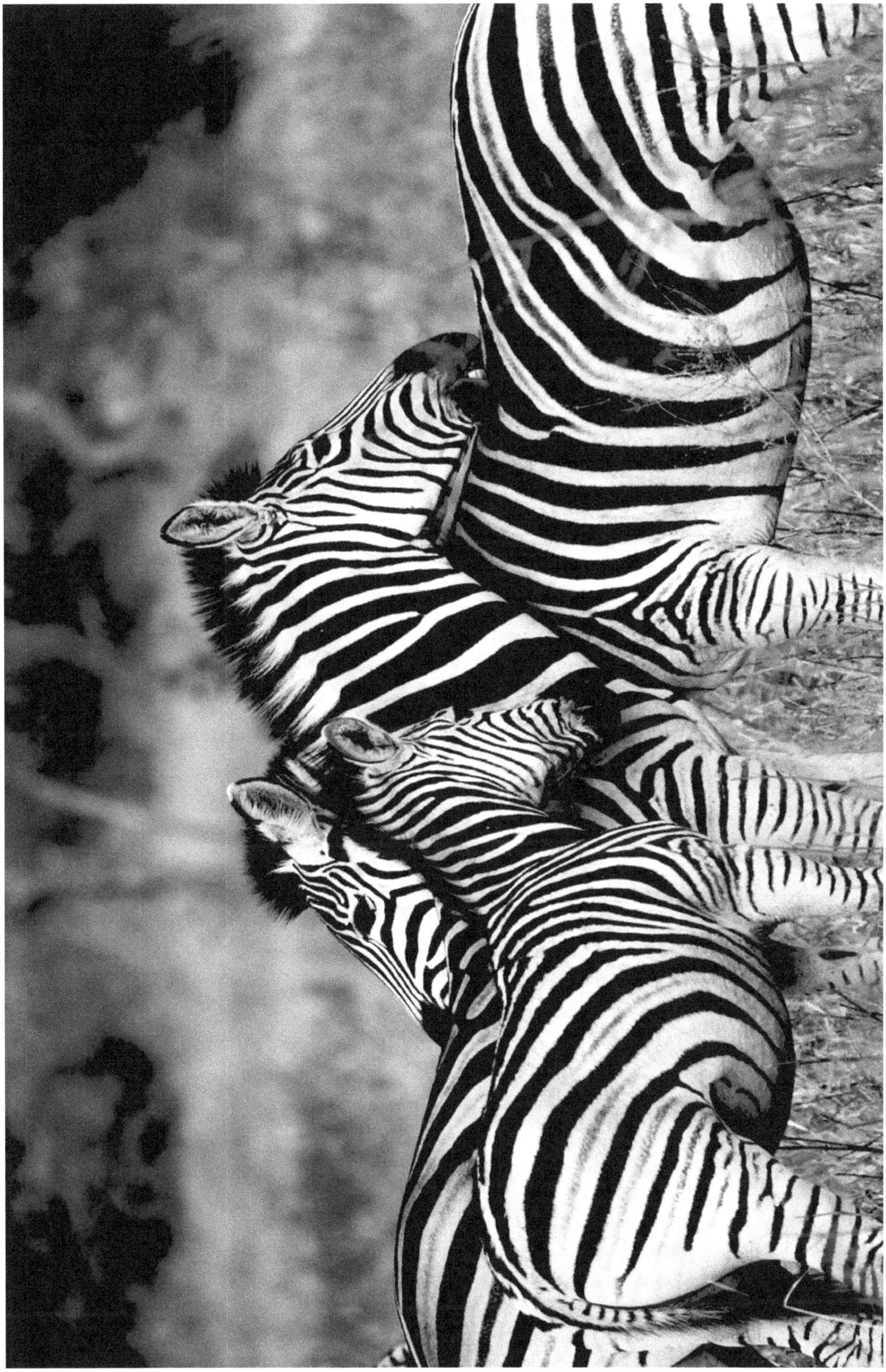

www.ingramcontent.com/pod-product-compliance
Lightning Source LLC
Chambersburg PA
CBHW081120280526
45787CB00007B/2913
* 9 7 8 1 5 3 5 1 2 1 2 2 4 *